UNSUNG HEROES
of Hispanic Heritage

ILEANA ROS-LEHTINEN

FIRST LATINA ELECTED TO U.S. CONGRESS

Tammy Gagne

Mitchell Lane

PUBLISHERS

2001 SW 31st Avenue
Hallandale, FL 33009
www.mitchelllane.com

First Edition, 2021.
Author: Tammy Gagne
Designer: Ed Morgan
Editor: Morgan Brody

Series: Unsung Heroes of Hispanic Heritage
Title: Ileana Ros-Lehtinen: First Latina Elected to U.S. Congress / by Tammy Gagne

Hallandale, FL : Mitchell Lane Publishers, [2021]

Library bound ISBN: 978-1-68020-669-2
eBook ISBN: 978-1-68020-670-8

PHOTO CREDITS: Design Elements, freepik.com, cover: ??, p. 5 Shutterstock, p. 7 public domain United States, p. 8 Shutterstock, p. 9 Shutterstock, p. 11 public domain United States, p. 13 DG/ Ileana Ros-Lehtinen Office/Newscom, p. 17 State Archives of Florida, p. 23 Associated Press, p. 25 COLIN BRALEY/REUTERS/Newscom, p. 27 State Archives of Florida, p. 29 Associated Press, p. 31 CARL JUSTE/TNS/Newscom, p. 33 Scott J. Ferrell/Congressional Quarterly/ Newscom, p. 35 CARL JUSTE/TNS/Newscom, p. 37 Associted Press, p. 39 Bill Clark/CQ Roll Call/Newscom, p. 41 Tom Williams/CQ Roll Call/Newscom,

CONTENTS

BEATING THE ODDS

"How was your first day of school?" Dad asked as Elisa and Markos climbed into their family's minivan.

"Great," Elisa said. "I think I'm going to run for student council."

"That's terrific," Dad said. But Markos just smirked. "What's the matter, son?"

"They served broccoli for lunch today—on pizza!" Markos replied. "And I think Elisa is wasting her time. She has no chance of winning. It's just a popularity contest. Sorry, sis." He hadn't meant to hurt her feelings.

It was true that Elisa wasn't the most popular student in the seventh grade. But she was just as smart as the other candidates. People who knew her also liked her.

"What do you think, Elisa?" Dad asked.

"I think my chances are as good as anybody else's," Elisa said. "I read a book for my summer reading challenge about Ileana Ros-Lehtinen. She was the first Latina to serve in Congress. She retired in 2018 after nearly 30 years in office." She addressed the last part to her brother. If he could imply she wasn't popular, she had no problem implying he didn't know anything about politics. "Many people didn't think she had much chance of winning her first election either. But she won."

"That's the right attitude," Dad said. "That's not the only thing you have in common with the congresswoman," he added. "Ros-Lehtinen was born in Cuba like Mima." Both Elisa and Markos loved Mima dearly. She too was retired now. But she became a teacher after moving to the United States. Mima was the reason they both loved books so much. She had read to them all the time when they were younger.

Ileana Ros-Lehtinen

"Ros-Lehtinen faced discrimination," Elisa told her brother. "When she ran for Congress, her opponent used the slogan, 'This is an American seat.' But voters realized how racist that was. They might not have known who she was at the start of the race, but they voted for her in the end. And I think people might vote for me, too."

"Wow, you're really serious about this, aren't you?" Markos asked.

"I sure am," she answered. "I've even chosen my first platform. If I am elected, I will make sure that broccoli is never served on school pizza again."

"Can I be your campaign manager?" Markos asked. He was joking. But Elisa knew he supported more than her stance on pizza toppings."

SAYING NO TO RACISM

Most candidates who run for Congress take part in debates before the election. But when Ileana Ros-Lehtinen ran against Gerald F. Richman, she would not take part in this exercise. She refused to appear on the same stage with him because of his racist campaign slogan.

CHAPTER TWO

2

A NEW HOME

Ileana Ros-Lehtinen in 1985

Ileana Carmen Ros was born about 100 miles from the United States in Havana, Cuba. She came into the world on July 15, 1952. When she was growing up, Cuba was ruled by a dictator named Fidel Castro. He did not respect basic human rights or freedom of speech. When people spoke out against his government, they were arrested. Some were even executed. Many Cubans fled the Communist nation during Castro's time in office. Ileana was just eight years old when her family escaped to the United States.

Her parents Enrique Emilio and Amanda Adato Ros made a new home for Ileana and her brother Henry in Miami, Florida. At first the family hoped to return to Cuba one day. With help from the U.S. government, about 1,400 Cubans who had escaped Cuba returned to the island in April of 1961. They tried to remove Castro from power in the Bay of Pigs invasion, but Castro's military was too strong. The invaders surrendered in less than a day. Enrique soon realized the United States was now his family's permanent home. He wanted his children to have a country of their own, so he vowed to raise them as loyal Americans.

But Ileana and Henry were still very young. They did not yet fully understand the many freedoms they now had in the United States. The first thing Ileana fell in love with about her new country was Halloween. In 2018, she Tweeted, "When my brother and I arrived in the U.S. so many years ago, we knew we were in paradise cause the kids went door to door and got candy!"

Ileana and her brother Henry enjoyed the same pastimes as other American children. They are seen here shortly after Henry broke his arm playing baseball.

Another thing that Ileana enjoyed was going to school. Although she spoke fluent Spanish, she especially enjoyed studying English. She loved learning so much in fact that she decided to pursue a career as a teacher. Following her graduation from Southwest High School, she went on to earn four college degrees. They included a Ph.D. in education from the University of Miami.

Ros put her education to good use educating others. In 1978, she founded a private elementary school in Hialeah, Florida. Eastern Academy was different from many other elementary schools of its time in an important way: It was bilingual. The teachers spoke both English and Spanish. This made a big difference for the children who attended the school.

Although Spanish was Miami-Dade County's second official language, some people thought that students should only speak English in U.S. schools. Some activists even fought to remove Spanish as an official language entirely. But Ros knew that Hispanic families needed Spanish-speaking schools. Kids who could not yet speak fluent English needed teachers they could understand. Ros fought for these kids to get the same education as those who already spoke English.

Learning can be difficult for kids who do not speak the same language as the teacher. Bilingual schools make a huge difference in their success in the classroom.

ONE STEP AT A TIME

Ros began as a teacher's assistant for Miami-Dade County Public schools. She then spent eight years at Eastern Academy where she also served as the school's principal.

Ros quickly became a person who got things done. When she saw a need, she filled it. Eastern Academy may never have existed without her commitment to education for all.

3

MAKING A DIFFERENCE IN DIFFERENT WAYS

Ros cared deeply about her students. As she got to know their families, parents often confided to her that money was among their biggest struggles. They wanted to send their kids to college so they could fulfill their own dreams. But many of them had a hard time just making ends meet. Large parts of their paychecks were going to taxes, which always seemed to be increasing. The parents had already seen the difference Ros had made in their children's education. Many of them told her she would

Ros is seen here in the 1980s.

also make a great politician. They thought she could make an even bigger difference in that job. Eventually they convinced her to run for the state's legislature.

In 1982, Ros was elected to the Florida House of Representatives. One of her biggest accomplishments there was the creation of the Florida Prepaid College Program. This plan helps Florida families afford in-state college tuition. This cost can rise significantly between the time children are born and when they are ready to enter college. But a prepaid program locks in a fixed rate. Through the plan, parents can start paying now without worrying about the cost changing later. In the years since its creation, Florida's Prepaid College Program has become the largest prepaid tuition program in the United States.

Serving in the Florida State House was changing Ros's life in more ways than one. While there, she met another state legislator, a lawyer named Dexter Lehtinen. The two quickly hit it off and decided to get married in 1984. The new couple also decided to run for State Senate, easily winning both seats. Neither of them would stay in the state legislature long, however. Dexter soon took a job as a U.S. attorney. Ileana was also seeking to serve a bigger role—as a U.S. Congresswoman.

Fellow state senators Ileana Ros-Lehtinen and
Dexter Lehtinen are seen here discussing an issue
in the Florida State Legislature.

Her victory in that race earned her a place in national history. The win made her the first Cuban American elected to the House. Ros-Lehtinen didn't even realize that she had also opened another important door for Latinas. She was in the middle of an interview with *Today Show* host Katie Couric when she found out. Couric asked her how it felt to become the first Hispanic woman to serve in the U.S. House of Representatives. "Wow, I guess it feels good!" Ros-Lehtinen replied.

Education remained one of her biggest focuses as a member of the U.S. House. She supported legislation to make financial aid available to more students. She also worked to help veterans receive money for college after serving in the U.S. military. She was still fighting for education, just in new ways.

Ileana Ros-Lehtinen screams with excitement upon hearing that she had won a seat in the U.S. Congress.

MANY FIRSTS

Ileana Ros-Lehtinen was the first Cuban American woman elected to both state legislatures in Florida.

Ros-Lehtinen continued to help others through her work in Congress. She is seen here with Arianne Horta, who nearly died coming to the United States on a boat from Cuba in 1999. U.S. reporters could not understand Horta, so Ros-Lehtinen translated for her.

CHAPTER FOUR

4

WORKING TOGETHER

Ros-Lehtinen was proud to be a trailblazer for other Hispanic American women. But she wasn't satisfied with simply opening doors. She wanted to do important work in Congress for the people of her district. She knew the best way to accomplish this goal was by working with the other representatives, regardless of their party. Ros-Lehtinen was a Republican. But she always kept an open mind when dealing with Democratic members of Congress. She didn't see the Democrats as the enemy; she saw the country's problems as the enemy. By working together, the legislators had a better chance of fixing those issues.

Voters responded to Ros-Lehtinen's efforts. They liked that she listened to what the people wanted instead of simply voting with the majority of Republicans. This is likely how she was elected 15 times by a largely Democratic district. She focused on the individual issues that were important to them. She saw her job as representing the viewpoints of her constituents. These are the people who live in a particular voting district.

One issue that Ros-Lehtinen agreed with many Democrats about was immigration. As someone who had come to the United States from Cuba, she understood the importance of welcoming people from other nations. She supported the creation of a path to citizenship for people who were in the United States illegally. This was the part of immigration reform that most Republicans and Democrats disagreed about most strongly. It is still being debated in the House.

Ros-Lehtinen is seen here embracing Francis Martinez. Her husband, Eusebio Penalver, was kept a prisoner in Cuba for 28 years for speaking out against Fidel Castro.

Another issue that became important to Ros-Lehtinen was LGBTQ rights. One of Ileana and Dexter's four children came to them during college, sharing that he identified as a transgender man. Although he had been born and raised as a girl named Amanda, he now wanted to be called Rodrigo. While many Americans respect the identities of trans people, they also face a large amount of discrimination. But Rodrigo received only support from his family.

In an interview with the CBS Miami television station, Ileana said, "As parents we wanted to make sure Rigo understood we were totally fine with it," she said. Their top priority was his safety. "Our society is sometimes not inviting and not caring enough and there is no mystery that LGBTQ kids when they are younger are bullied."

Ros-Lehtinen spoke out for the rights of LGBTQ people during her time in Congress. In 2012, she was also the first Republican in Congress to support same-sex marriage. Her willingness to speak her mind instead of following a party line earned her the respect of many voters and fellow politicians.

Ros-Lehtinen and her husband show support for their transgendered son, Rodrigo, through a PSA called "Family is Everything." Its purpose is to stop discrimination against LGBTQ people.

HEADING A HOUSE COMMITTEE

During her time in office, Ros-Lehtinen became the first woman to chair the House Committee on Foreign Affairs. She quickly gained a reputation for opposing oppressive governments like the one she had grown up with in Cuba.

Ros-Lehtinen is seen here with fellow Republican and Democratic members of Congress as they discuss legislation about war powers and U.S. involvement in Libya. Like Cuba, this nation has a history of oppressing its people.

A LASTING IMPRESSION

Ros-Lehtinen talks with well-wishers after announcing her retirement from Congress in 2017.

After nearly 30 years in Congress, Ros-Lehtinen announced that she would not seek re-election in 2018. In an interview with the *Miami Herald*, she said that her favorite memories from her time in Congress would be of her constituents. She deeply enjoyed meeting many of them and hoped they thought she had done a good job. "I can never repay what this country has given me," she said, "and I'm honored to have been South Florida's voice in Congress for so many years."

Although she would soon leave office, many other politicians vowed to continue fighting for the issues that Ros-Lehtinen believes in so deeply. Senator Marco Rubio, a fellow Republican lawmaker from Florida, shares Ros-Lehtinen's strong stance against communist governments. Before running for office himself, Rubio had been one of Ros-Lehtinen's interns many years earlier. He too was now known as a moderate Republican, often crossing the aisle to get things done with his fellow U.S. senators from both parties.

Ros-Lehtinen's own voice was not silenced after her last term in the House. After ending her career in Congress, Ros-Lehtinen returned to her first passion: teaching. But this time she would be doing it at the college level. She and her husband decided to co-teach a political science class at the University of Miami.

Ros-Lehtinen helped pave the way for other members of the Senate to cross the aisle to work with members of the Democratic party. She is seen here with U.S. Senator Marco Rubio, who is also known as a moderate Republican.

Students flocked to the class to learn about government from someone who had actually served at one of the highest levels in the nation. One such student, Denisse Sandoval, told school's online newspaper News@TheU, "There was no way I was going to pass up this opportunity. She is a great role model for all of us women."

Ros-Lehtinen made a lasting impression on the other members of Congress, as well. After her exit, her fellow lawmakers named a bill after the retired congresswoman. The Ileana Ros-Lehtinen United States-Israel Security Assistance Authorization Act set aside $3.3 billion for security assistance for the war-torn country. Ros-Lehtinen had worked hard to strengthen the relationship between Israel and the United States during her time on the House Committee on Foreign Affairs. This made the bill's name especially meaningful to her.

Ros-Lehtinen is seen here doing what she loves most—talking to students—on the steps of the Capitol Building.

Her story is a fine example of just what a person can accomplish as a citizen of the United States. But Ros-Lehtinen does not take the credit. Instead, she gives it to her beloved adopted nation. As she told *The Jerusalem Post* back in 2010, "When we first came over here, I was eight and I didn't know a word of English, and here I am a member of Congress . . . It says a lot, not about me but about the opportunities available in this country."

Ros-Lehtinen and House Minority Leader Nancy Pelosi are seen here in 2018 during the Washington Press Club Foundation's annual dinner. The two women belong to different parties, but they do not let that stop them from working together—or enjoying events such as this one.

CONTINUING THE TRADITION

In 2018, Democrat Donna Shalala won the congressional seat that Ros-Lehtinen gave up. Following the election, Ros-Lehtinen wished her well with a gift for her office—a Cuban coffee maker. Serving the South Florida beverage to staff members had become a tradition of sorts during her time in office.

Throughout Ros-Lehtinen's long career, she has advocated for women in the military, education for all, LGBTQ rights, and for marriage equality. Her efforts have helped shape the United States.

Ros-Lehtinen wished Democrat Donna Shalala the best of luck when she took over the Republican's seat in Congress.

TIMELINE

1952   Ileana Ros is born in Havana, Cuba on July 15.

1960   Her parents escape the Communist island nation and settle in Miami, Florida.

1982   Ros becomes the first Cuban American woman elected to the Florida House of Representatives.

1984   She marries fellow state legislator Dexter Lehtinen.

1987   Ileana Ros-Lehtinen becomes the first Cuban American woman elected to the Florida Senate.

1989   She becomes the first Cuban American and the first Hispanic woman to serve in the U.S. House of Representatives.

2011   Ros-Lehtinen becomes the first woman to chair the House Committee on Foreign Affairs.

2012   Ros-Lehtinen becomes the first Republican to support marriage equality.

She also became the first Republican in the House to support same-sex marriage.

2017   She announces that she will not seek re-election in the 2018 race for Congress.

FIND OUT MORE

Biographical Directory of the United States Congress. Ileana Ros-Lehtinen. http://bioguide.congress.gov/scripts/biodisplay. pl?index=R000435

Cooper, Ilene. *A Woman in the House (and Senate)*. New York: Abrams Books for Young Readers, 2014.

Lopez, Silvia. *Ileana Ros-Lehtinen* (Spanish edition). CreateSpace, 2016.

PBS. Cuban Exiles in America. https://www.pbs.org/wgbh/americanexperience/ features/castro-cuban-exiles-america/

United States House of Representatives. Women of Color in Congress. https://history.house.gov/Exhibitions-and-Publications/ WIC/Historical-Data/Women-of-Color-in-Congress/

WORKS CONSULTED

_____. "Bay of Pigs Invasion." The History Channel, June 6, 2019. https://www.history.com/topics/cold-war/bay-of-pigs-invasion

_____. "Florida Prepaid College Plan." University of Florida. https://www.sfa.ufl.edu/florida-prepaid-college-plan/

Anapol, Avery. "Here's how politicians celebrated Halloween." *The Hill*, November 1, 2018. https://thehill.com/blogs/in-the-know/in-the-know/414228-heres-how-politicians-celebrated-halloween

Anderson, Ashlee. "Ileana Ros-Lehtinen." National Women's History Museum, 2018. https://www.womenshistory.org/education-resources/biographies/ileana-ros-lehtinen

Clarke, Sara. "10 Things You Didn't Know About Ileana Ros-Lehtinen." *U.S. News & World Report*, May 4, 2017. https://www.usnews.com/news/national-news/articles/2017-05-04/10-things-you-didnt-know-about-ileana-ros-lehtinen

Daugherty, Alex. "Miami's 'big bad wolf' finishes a 29-year run in Congress." *Miami Herald*, December 9, 2019. https://www.miamiherald.com/news/politics-government/article222806080.html

Daugherty, Alex. "The perks of retirement: House to vote on a bill named after Ileana Ros-Lehtinen." *Miami Herald*, September 12, 2018. https://miamiherald.typepad.com/nakedpolitics/2018/09/the-perks-of-retirement-house-to-vote-on-a-bill-named-after-ileana-ros-lehtinen.html

DeFede, Jim. "Ileana's Son: From Amanda to Rodrigo." CBS Miami, November 17, 2014. https://miami.cbslocal.com/2014/11/17/ileanas-son-from-amanda-to-rodrigo/

Gamboa, Suzanne. "Retiring this year, Ileana Ros-Lehtinen, first Latina in Congress, defies stereotypes." NBC News, April 11, 2018. https://www.nbcnews.com/news/latino/retiring-year-ileana-ros-lehtinen-first-latina-congress-defied-stereotypes-n864456

Gutierrez, Barbara. "Ileana Ros-Lehtinen returns to the classroom." News@TheU, February 2019. https://news.miami.edu/stories/2019/02/ileana-ros-lehtinen-returns-to-the-classroom.html

Krieger, Hilary Leila. "Ileana Ros-Lehtinen: Ready to Play Hard Ball." *The Jerusalem Post*, December 23, 2010. https://www.jpost.com/Features/In-Thespotlight/Ileana-Ros-Lehtinen-Ready-to-play-hardball

Mazzei, Patricia. "Ileana Ros-Lehtinen to retire from Congress." *Miami Herald*, May 1, 2017. https://www.miamiherald.com/news/local/community/miami-dade/article147718764.html

O'Connor, Bill. "First Latina Congresswoman Ileana Ros-Lehtinen Announces Retirement." *Hip Latina*, May 1, 2017. https://hiplatina.com/ileana-ros-lehtinen-first-latina-congress/

Ros-Lehtinen, Ileana. "Why I'm retiring from Congress. A message from Ileana Ros-Lehtinen." *Miami Herald*. https://www.miamiherald.com/news/politics-government/article147724204.html

Smiley, David. "The Life and Times of Ileana Ros-Lehtinen." *Miami Herald*, Updated May 1, 2017. https://www.miamiherald.com/news/local/community/miami-dade/article147751899.html

Soto, Luis Feldstein. "The day Ileana Ros-Lehtinen was elected to Congress." *Miami Herald*, April 30, 2017. https://www.miamiherald.com/news/politics-government/article147721324.html

Vasquez, Michael. "How Ros-Lehtinen found a way to connect with Jews, Hispanics and everyone else." *Miami Herald*, Updated April 30, 2017. https://www.miamiherald.com/news/politics-government/article147721574.html

INDEX

ABOUT THE AUTHOR

Tammy Gagne has written more than 200 books for both adults and children. Among her favorites have been titles about people from different cultures with great passion for their life and work. *Ileana Ros-Lehtinen* is one such book. Others include *Mario Molina* and *Sylvia Mendez*. Gagne lives in northern New England with her husband, son, and a menagerie of pets.